D1282857

Our World of Water

Rivers

Arthur Best

Cavendish
Square

New York

Published in 2018 by Cavendish Square Publishing, LLC
243 5th Avenue, Suite 136, New York, NY 10016

Copyright © 2018 by Cavendish Square Publishing, LLC

First Edition

Cataloging-in-Publication Data

Names: Best, Arthur, author.
Title: Rivers / Arthur Best.
Description: New York : Cavendish Square, 2018. | Series: Our world of water | Includes index.
Identifiers: ISBN 9781502630988 (pbk.) | ISBN 9781502631008 (library bound) | ISBN 9781502630995 (6 pack) | ISBN 9781502631015 (ebook)
Subjects: LCSH: Rivers--Juvenile literature.
Classification: LCC GB1203.8 B47 2018 | DDC 551.48'3--dc23

Editorial Director: David McNamara
Copy Editor: Nathan Heidelberger
Associate Art Director: Amy Greenan
Designer: Alan Sliwinski
Production Coordinator: Karol Szymczuk
Photo Research: J8 Media

The photographs in this book are used by permission and through the courtesy of: Miks Mihails Ignats/Shutterstock.com; p. 5 Iness Arna/Shutterstock.com; p. 7 Elizabeth Hooley/Shutterstock.com; p. 9 Jason Patrick Ross/Shutterstock.com; p. 11 Education Images/UIG/Getty Images; p. 13 Photolinc/Shutterstock.com; p. 15 Arisa J/Shutterstock.com; p. 17 Jon666/iStock/Thinkstock; p. 19 Yupa Watchanakit/Shutterstock.com; p. 21 Frantic00/Shutterstock.com.

Printed in the United States of America

Contents

Rivers are made of moving water.

Rivers carry freshwater.

Rivers get their water from rain.

The water flows down the land into the river.

Rivers can get their water from lakes.

Rivers can flow through lakes.

Two rivers can join to make a bigger river.

All water flows downhill.

Rivers empty into the ocean.

The end of a river is called the **mouth**.

11

The sun heats water in the ocean.

Some water **evaporates**.

It goes into the air.

The water **vapor** makes clouds.

The clouds rain onto land.

This gives more water for rivers!

This is called the water **cycle**.

15

Many animals live in rivers.

Otters live in rivers.

Turtles live in rivers.

Catfish live in rivers.

Cattails grow in rivers.

So does **duckweed**.

A duckweed plant looks like a tiny, floating leaf!

19

People drink water that comes from rivers.

We need rivers to keep water moving in our world!

21

New Words

cycle (SY-kul) Something that repeats.

duckweed (DUCK-weed) A small, floating plant.

evaporates (e-VAH-puh-rayts) Turns to steam.

mouth (MOWTH) The end of a river at the sea.

vapor (VAY-pur) Steam.

Index

23

About the Author

Arthur Best lives in Wisconsin with his wife and son. He has written many other books for children. He has kayaked on many rivers.

About

Bookworms help independent readers gain reading confidence through high-frequency words, simple sentences, and strong picture/text support. Each book explores a concept that helps children relate what they read to the world they live in.

11-18

EMMA S. CLARK MEMORIAL LIBRARY
SETAUKET, NEW YORK 11733

To view your account,
renew or request an item,
visit www.emmaclark.org